THE COMPLETE HISTORY OF NEW ZEALAND (IN LESS THAN TWO HOURS)

PETER JESSUP

HURRICANE PRESS

Published by Hurricane Press
Cambridge, New Zealand
© *Peter Jessup*

All rights reserved. No part of this publication may be reproduced, stored in a retrieval system, or transmitted in any form or by any means, electronic, mechanical, photocopying, recording or otherwise, without the prior permission of the publishers and copyright holders.

Cover image: © Andy Heyward | Dreamstime.com

FOREWORD

THOUGH NEW ZEALAND is regarded as a relatively 'young' country, it has a fascinating history. For a small nation it has quickly earned its place in the world, through its active involvement in international affairs, its reputation for innovation and friendliness and not least its willingness to influence global thinking.

It was the first country in the world to give women the right to vote. It established principles of social welfare envied and copied elsewhere. It created a nuclear-free zone around its shores. I have attempted to tell New Zealand's story in a concise fashion, so it can be appreciated in no more than two hours.

I hope I've done it justice.

— *Peter Jessup*

INTRODUCTION

NEW ZEALAND is a multi-cultural society with a democratically elected government and an economy based on exports of dairy products, meat and wool, wood, seafood and horticulture. Tourism and providing education for overseas students also make significant contributions to the economy.

The country's population of more than 5 million is concentrated in relatively few urban areas and hence vast areas are sparsely populated.

The land mass of New Zealand's two main islands exceeds 268,000 square kilometres, meaning it is 10% larger than the United Kingdom and about the same size as Colorado in the United States.

Much of the landscape resembles features of other countries — the southern fiords are like those in Norway, the ski fields are reminiscent of Colorado, while the hot pools and geysers would be familiar to visitors from Iceland.

We have areas of near-desert like those in the middle states of North America, white sand like the beaches of Australia and sub-tropical rainforests similar to those in Fiji.

Nearly 15% of the land mass is invested in National Parks

and other conservation areas where housing and industry are not allowed.

Activities that attract guests from around the world include whale and dolphin-watching and trips to the many offshore islands.

Skiing attracts visitors to Mt Ruapehu in the North Island and along the backbone of the Southern Alps in the South Island, where numerous skifields are within easy driving distance of each other.

Visitors can experience adventure sports including white and blackwater rafting, bungy jumping (which was invented in New Zealand), jet boating up narrow river gorges, paragliding and more.

The freshwater trout and offshore game fishing are world-class, as are the diving and surfing.

Most Kiwis are sports enthusiasts. As well as the national game of rugby union, there is strong support for rugby league, football, basketball, netball, cricket and yachting. The nation has produced world champions in sports from athletics to motor racing.

Visitor surveys confirm New Zealanders are a friendly bunch.

A straight face and a quip that some might consider surly and intimidating is most likely the Kiwi cultural test of 'taking the Mickey', 'pulling your chain' or 'just having a go at ya, mate.'

But it's taken hundreds of years to shape the New Zealand landscape and the character of its people.

Since the Maori arrived more than 600 years ago and European settlers followed in the 19th century, New Zealanders have worked hard to establish their own sense of identity, gradually moving away from the influence of Britain during the 20th century.

The Kiwi culture evolved as immigrants continued to influence everything from food to language.

The vast number of restaurants throughout the country bear testimony to the diversity of the flavours we claim as our own. Indian restaurants, for instance, offer 'hot' or 'New Zealand hot' curries.

A fifth of all current New Zealand residents were not born in the country; they chose this place as their home.

The country has a reputation for celebrating diversity, and for tolerance.

And while this book provides the story of how today's New Zealand came about, spare a thought for its future.

New Zealanders are among the world's most enthusiastic travellers with more than half a million Kiwis either living or travelling abroad at any time. They are learning new ways and ideas, ready to return home to continue the shaping of their nation.

Chapter One

GEOGRAPHY, FLORA AND FAUNA

THE NEW ZEALAND land mass was once part of a mighty southern continent known as Gondwanaland, which included Australia, South Africa, South America and India.

Over millennia, tectonic plate movement separated the various countries. New Zealand was the last to break away, between 70 and 80 million years ago and, as the youngest, continues to experience violent upheavals from the earth's core in the form of volcanic eruptions and earthquakes.

The country sits on the boundaries of the Pacific Plate as it grinds against and over-rides the Indo-Australia Plate. Scientists describe this movement as occurring at the rate that fingernails grow.

Over time, tension builds and is released in the form of earthquakes such as those in Christchurch in 2010 and 2011.

Hence, New Zealand has the nickname 'The Shaky Isles.'

In the centre of the North Island is Lake Taupo, 616 square kms of water up to 186 metres deep, which sits in the volcanic cone formed as a result of one of the largest eruptions ever on the planet.

Taupo first erupted 30,000 years ago, before the time of man, and again 1,800 years ago, an event recorded by Chinese and Italian historians who wrote about the reddening of the sky.

The latter eruption was twice the size of the eruption of Mt St Helens in the United States in 1980.

In 1886, Mt Tarawera, near Rotorua, erupted, sending smoke and ash around the Southern Hemisphere.

The lava flow buried what was regarded as a world treasure, the Pink and White Terraces, formed over centuries by hot mineral waters colouring the rock of a series of small waterfalls.

Active volcanoes include Mt Ruapehu just south of Taupo in the central North Island, and White Island, offshore from Whakatane. Auckland is the site of 50 volcanic cones, some of which have been excavated to provide the bluestone hard rock used to build early city buildings and cobbled streets. Scoria, which is a light rock from air-blown lava, is used for roading and drainage.

Rangitoto Island, which attracts many tourists, is a good example of Auckland's volcanic cones. Most of Auckland's volcanoes are monogynetic, meaning they erupted just once, though some eruptions lasted up to 10 years.

Scientists believe Auckland will experience further volcano activity at some point in the future, most likely from a new source.

Rangitoto

Rangitoto is the likeliest of Auckland's existing volcanoes to erupt again but scientists have no idea when this might occur.

Scientists have proved that more than 200 million years ago, during the Ice Age, the planet experienced about 30 major oscillations in global temperature, the most recent of which affected New Zealand.

The fiords of the South Island and the Canterbury Plains and its river basins were formed by glacial action.

About 12,000 years ago, as temperatures rose, broadleaf forest began to take over the glacial plains and 7,000 years ago, the entire country was covered by rainforest.

The fossils of dinosaur bones have been found in caves in Otago and Hawkes Bay. It is believed the large predators became extinct during the freezing periods. New Zealand's isolation since means the wildlife is limited and unusual.

The country has no land mammals except for three species of cave bat. The 25 species of freshwater fish are all small, the biggest being 10cm in length.

Many of the bird species were flightless because there were no predators to attack them until the arrival of man.

Early Maori burned forests to scare birds into nets and

traps and in this fashion the moa, similar to the ostrich or emu, was made extinct. The deforestation was extreme and at least 30 other mostly flightless species disappeared.

European hunters in the early 19th century quickly accounted for another great bird, the Haast eagle, which had a bigger wingspan (three metres) than any other eagle in the world.

The most recognised of New Zealand's birdlife is the kiwi, which is found nationwide in the wild but is endangered in many areas due to attacks from dogs as well as stoats and weasels which eat the bird's eggs.

The flightless kiwi became the national symbol of New Zealand after its image was adopted by military regiments in the late 19th century, and by a manufacturer of shoe polish some years later.

The pukeko, or swamp hen, is common, with its stunning blue plumage and red beak a stand-out on many waterways.

The takehe, weka, kokako and kakapo are rare but can be seen in the wild and on island reserves where efforts are being made to strengthen their populations.

In the forest you will hear the twittering of fantails and the melodic song of the tui, the bird that Maori legend deems to be a coward because of the white feathers at its throat.

The tui imitates the more songful bellbird, smaller and hard to spot.

The kea is an endemic parrot from the South Island high country, though fewer than 5,000 are believed to exist.

At the beach you will see gannets diving from on high to eat small fish, the long red-beaked oystercatcher which eats shellfish, the shag which swims powerfully underwater to chase fish and, in the right places, penguins which migrate to the sea and back every day.

Due to the lack of wild animals, early settlers introduced many species for food. Goats and pigs were set free on offshore islands so shipwrecked sailors would have something to eat.

Along with the easily controlled domestic cows and sheep came uncontrollable rabbits and possums, now regarded as pests.

Pheasants, ducks, geese, swans and quails were imported in the early 1800s to provide meat and for sports shooting as were the more exotic Himalayan tahr and Canadian moose.

In 1861, the government passed The Protection of Certain Animals Act ruling that: 'No deer of any kind, hare, swan, partridge, English plover, rook, starling, thrush or blackbird' could be shot for the rest of the decade.

Three years later, the Wild Birds Protection Act stated: 'No wild duck, paradise duck, or pigeon indigenous in the colony shall be hunted, taken, or killed except during the months of April, May, June, and July in any year.'

Salmon and trout were introduced to waterways, and were protected by a law passed in 1867. They have thrived.

The English desire to reproduce their countryside resulted in the unfortunate introduction of gorse and boxthorn in the early 1800s. While these are trimmed as hedges in cold northern climates, they grow out of control across untended land in warmer New Zealand temperatures.

To complete the hedgerows, the English settlers brought hedgehogs (in 1870) as well as sparrows, mynas, blackbirds and thrushes.

Weasels and stoats were introduced in 1885 to control rabbits but instead took to birds and are regarded today as pests.

After its haphazard beginnings, New Zealand became increasingly aware of the need to protect its wildlife and natural environment during the 20th century.

In 1901, the Noxious Weeds Act was introduced and soon

after a commission was appointed with the brief of preserving scenery.

In 1923, the Royal Forest and Bird Protection Society of New Zealand was formed to conserve indigenous plant and wildlife.

In 1941, The Soil and Rivers Control Act was enforced to become the first piece of co-ordinated environmental law in New Zealand.

In 1986, The Environment Act established the Ministry for the Environment and the Office of the Parliamentary Commissioner for the Environment. The Commissioner is appointed for five-year terms, to provide independent checks on the system of environmental management and the performance of public authorities on environmental matters.

The same year, the country implemented a Quota Management System (QMS) to control and protect stocks of fish within New Zealand waters. It was the first fishing management system of its type to be implemented anywhere in the world.

Chapter Two
SETTLEMENT

EXACTLY HOW and when Maori came to New Zealand remains subject to speculation because no written record exists. Historians believe they arrived from Polynesia between 600 and 700 years ago.

Maori tradition tells of the explorer Kupe finding what he called Aotearoa — 'The Land of the Long White Cloud' — which is how the country often appears from the sea.

Migration was presumably driven by the burgeoning populations on small Pacific Islands that could not provide enough food.

The newcomers brought foods including the sweet potato (kumara) and animals, including the rat kiore. Legend has it that Maori can trace their ancestry to one of seven canoes made of planks lashed together, with sails of woven fibre: The Aotea, Arawa, Kurahaupo, Mataatua, Tainui, Takitimu or the Tokomaru.

New Zealand iwi (Maori tribes)

Different tribes (iwi) laid claim to different areas, the major ones being Ngapuhi in Northland/Auckland, Tainui in the Waikato, Te Arawa in the Bay of Plenty, Ngati Porou on East Cape, Te Ati Awa from Taranaki to Wellington, while Ngai Tahu inhabited the whole of the South Island.

More than 6,000 settlements were built around the country and remains exist of more than 500 fortified hills (known as pa) where local people would gather in defence when attacked by other tribes.

. They grew potatoes, corn and vines in stone-fenced gardens, gathered seafood and stored it by drying and salting it, and boiled the roots of flaxes, cabbage trees and ferns.

They used stone adzes to carve intricate panels and poles for their buildings and canoes (known as waka) built for food-gathering trips.

The Dutchman Abel Tasman, for whom the Tasman Sea is named, was the first European to chart any of New Zealand

and he moored in Golden Bay on the northern tip of the South Island in 1642.

Four sailors rowing to shore were brutally killed, prompting Tasman to up anchor without ever setting foot on land.

In 1769, Captain James Cook sailed the Endeavour on a voyage of exploration in the South Pacific and on October 6 a lookout named Young Nick sighted land at Hawkes Bay, where a headland remains named for him.

Cook spent much time interacting with Maori and returned to New Zealand in 1770 and 1773 aboard the Resolution to continue charting the country's coastline and to observe the Transit of Venus to help establish accurate navigational measurements.

The first regular European visitors were whalers and sealers in the early 1800s and their work was originally concentrated in the deep south, including the Chatham Islands where they found the Moriori people, assumed to be distant relatives of Maori.

In 1835, the Maori tribe Te Ati Awa invaded and overran the Moriori, killing as many as 3,000 and enslaving others.

Christian missionaries were among the first settlers on the mainland and their early recording of history provides the majority of information on the meeting between Maori and Europeans.

By 1838, the population was estimated to consist of 80,000 Maori and 1,000 non–Maori.

By 1840, the British government, seeking land for settlers, called Maori chiefs together at Waitangi in the Bay of Islands and asked them to negotiate what became known as the Treaty of Waitangi which remains valid today.

Arguments and land occupations continue as a result of the differing meanings each side placed on the wording of the document.

Article One of the treaty states that Maori transfer the sovereignty of New Zealand to the British Crown.

Article Two states that Maori are forever guaranteed authority over their land and resources.

Article Three grants Maori all the rights and privileges of a British subject.

The government-sponsored New Zealand Company began rapidly buying land and at one stage claimed to have purchased a third of all of the country, a claim later found to be vastly exaggerated by its purchasing officers. But the company did promote the migration of more than 9,000 people by 1843.

Tamati Waka Nene, one of the signatories to the Treaty of Waitangi.

Generally, the settlers did not understand the Maori concept of communal land ownership and Maori did not understand that selling land often meant it would be clear-felled and fenced off.

As the expanding European population extended its influence beyond the early settlements, conflict escalated, survey pegs were pulled out and buildings burned.

In 1843, 22 colonists were killed in a land dispute at Wairau in Nelson.

In 1844, the northern chief Hone Heke cut down the flagpole that flew the British ensign above the then-main centre of Kororareka (now Russell) in the Bay of Islands. It was re-erected and Heke cut it down again, and later cut it down a third time to show Maori grievance with the land sales process.

In 1845, Maori took over Kororareka, sparking the first all-out battles and the sending of troops from England and its colonies. They stayed until 1865, and for much of that time comprised the largest overseas contingent of troops in the British Empire.

Maori showed a great propensity for trench warfare and inflicted heavy casualties when attacked in their pa, slipping away through hidden exits.

By 1858, several tribes had gathered under the Kingitangi (the King Movement) to present a united front to oppose expansion of European settlement.

Fighting started in Taranaki in 1860 and spread to Whanganui. Furious battles were fought at Rangiriri and Orakau in the Waikato in 1862 as the British marched south from their stronghold in Auckland, building the Great South Road to open more country for settlement.

A great battle took place at Gate Pa in the Bay of Plenty in 1864. East Coast, Hawkes Bay and Central North Island Maori gathered behind the prophet and chief Te Kooti to fight a prolonged war in the middle of the island.

Some Maori tribes remained loyal to the Crown and some took the opportunity to fight long-time opponents.

In return they were gifted land confiscated from 'rebels' and other land taken as punishment was vested in Crown interests, including the New Zealand Company. These issues remain subject of grievances to this day.

The wars also led to the rise of a Maori/Christian spirituality, though this too was misunderstood by the European settlers (known to Maori as Pakeha).

Te Kooti's house.

Te Kooti established the Ringatu faith. Te Kooti, Rua Kenana of the Ratana faith and the chief Te Whiti from Taranaki espoused peace through the Pai Marire ('good and peaceful') movement.

Its followers gathered around

a carved pole or po to sing and dance. They became known by Pakeha as 'Hauhau' which was the last, repeated word of their main song or 'karakia'.

The term Hauhau was, to Europeans, synonymous with civil disobedience, anti-European sentiment and violence. The Ringatu and Ratana faiths continue to exist today.

The rich pastoral land and the discovery of gold at Gabriel's Gully in Otago in 1861 and on the Coromandel Peninsula in 1862 ensured a steady flow of migrants. The Pakeha population doubled in the three years from 1861–1864.

Gradually, Maori opposition was swamped and fell away, not least because the Maori population was declining at a rapid rate as they succumbed to diseases and infections including simple influenza to which they had no immunity.

Farmers broke in land across the country and towns were built to support the rural base.

Major cities were established on harbours where sailing ships berthed to bring more settlers and return to foreign ports with agricultural produce.

Chapter Three

PRODUCE AND INCOME

AFTER THE WHALERS and sealers decimated the populations of marine mammals through the early 1800s, agriculture became the backbone of the country's earnings as settlers cleared land.

By 1879, the country had 13 million sheep and the country was exporting 28,000 tonnes of wool, mostly to Britain.

In 1882, the ship Dunedin took the world's first cargo of frozen meat carcasses to England. This prompted an extraordinary boom in sheep and cattle farming, with abattoirs being established throughout the country.

By the 1890s, businesses formed to profit from timber, with the straight bole of the kauri tree becoming prized for ship spars and its worm-resistant timber making it desirable for boatbuilding.

The kauri forests flourished north of the Waikato due to favourable climates, but were stripped by loggers. Production peaked at more than 100 million tonnes in 1903 but soon after the industry folded when all the easily-accessed timber was taken.

Surveying of non-coastal land led to findings of gold, coal and other minerals.

Each of these booms influenced the make-up of New Zealand's population. Chinese came for the 'gold rush' and more than 5,000 lived in the Otago region by the late 1860s.

Croatians from the seaside province of Dalmatia settled in large numbers to work in the kauri milling industry and then to dig for the gum that seeped into the ground as trees were removed.

Coal miners came from the north of England and Wales.

But farming remained the country's biggest earner and over time the expansion of meat processing resulted in large scale movement of Maori from the country to towns and cities to work in the industry.

The country was said to be 'living on the sheep's back' as farmers took to breeding sheep and selling their wool to Britain and the United States.

In 1951, as a result of the Korean War, the United States set out to create large stockpiles of wool, buying whatever New Zealand could provide. Wool prices tripled overnight.

In the 1960s, 65% of New Zealand's exports went to the United Kingdom as the British continued to enjoy New Zealand lamb for their Sunday roast meal, and consumed our butter and cheese.

Sensing this relationship with Britain would not last forever, New Zealand began building trade relationships with countries not so far away. A trade pact was signed with Japan in 1962 and three years later, the first steps to free trade with Australia were taken with the signing of the New Zealand–Australia Free Trade Agreement (NAFTA).

When Britain joined the European Economic Community in 1973, New Zealand lost its preferential treatment in UK markets and export earnings plummeted, while foreign debt grew alarmingly.

As the country learned to produce new products for different markets in the 1980s, the sheep population fell from its peak of more than 80 million to fewer than 40 million in the new millennium. As well as facing more competition for exported lamb, synthetics have increasingly replaced wool in clothing and carpets.

Farmers began to diversify, producing specialist meats such as venison, more grain crops, vegetables, timber and fruit including grapes for wine.

In 1982, New Zealand agreed terms with Australia for Closer Economic Relations (CER), leading to completely free access to each other's markets by 1988.

By 1984, Japan had overtaken Britain as a customer for New Zealand exported goods.

The Labour Government of 1984 removed state subsidies to farmers and governments have since required State Owned Enterprises such as power companies to return dividends.

Many industries have been deregulated, privatised or both. These include telecommunications, post, radio, taxis and liquor outlets, while import regulations have been significantly relaxed.

The floating of the New Zealand dollar in 1985, and the reduction in import tariffs, led to a rapid increase in the number of goods imported, leading to the reduction or closure of local manufacturing plants. For instance, the New Zealand motor manufacturing industry all but disappeared while demand soared for imported new and second hand cars from Japan.

The new prosperity is in dairying, to meet rapidly growing demand in the expanding economies of India and China.

New Zealand supplies about a third of the world's dairy products through the farmer-owned cooperative company Fonterra.

Recent governments have tried to promote a 'knowledge

economy' based on development and manufacture of high technology, with limited success.

Education has become an important income stream and by 2010, it had become the country's 6th biggest earner of overseas funds as tertiary institutions actively recruit foreign students and charge them fees.

Marine seabed areas have been opened up for use for aquaculture and forecasters say seafood exports could grow to $2.3 billion a year by 2022. The growth will come from an escalation of mussel, paua and oyster farming, and the extension of finfish farming from salmon to snapper, kingfish and hapuka.

Since the commercialisaton of air travel in the 1960s, tourism has increasingly played a major role in New Zealand's economy.

By 2010, tourism had become a $20 billion a year industry, providing one in 10 jobs, 10% of GDP and more than 18% of total export earnings.

As the nation entered its second decade of the new millennium, its main customers for exports were Australia (23%), United States (10%), China (10%), Japan (9%), other Asian countries (9%), Europe (7%), Middle East (7%), Britain (6%), India (6%), Russia (4%), South America (3%), Pacific Islands (2%).

Chapter Four
GOVERNANCE

NEW ZEALAND'S parliamentary system is based on the Westminster administration of Britain but is different structurally, as it has just one House rather than an upper and lower chamber.

This system was adopted after the British Crown gained agreement in 1840 from various Maori tribes to rule as sovereign in return for the protection of the Crown and the guarantee of the rights of a British subject for all citizens equally, as stated in the Treaty of Waitangi.

The Crown appointed Irish–born naval officer William Hobson as the Lieutenant–Governor of New Zealand in 1839 and he was sent to the Bay of Islands in January 1840.

After the signing of the Treaty on February 6, he proclaimed British Sovereignty on May 21.

Hobson read the charter proclaiming New Zealand a separate Crown Colony on May 3, 1841, and immediately took the Oath as its Governor. New Zealand's first capital was Kororareka (Russell) in the Bay of Islands. Hobson moved the capital to Auckland in January 1841. He died in Auckland in September 1842, aged 49.

Governor William Hobson.
Photo: Public domain.

The first significant election held in New Zealand took place in 1842 to decide representatives of the first Wellington Town council.

In 1843, Captain Robert Fitz-Roy, of the Royal Navy, was appointed Governor, with the brief of overseeing the implementation of the Treaty of Waitangi. But during his two-year term, land sale disputes escalated as large numbers of British settlers arrived and armed skirmishes broke out. FitzRoy was deemed to be ineffective at settling the disputes and he was replaced by Governor George Grey who held the role from 1845 till 1853.

In 1852, the British government passed the New Zealand Constitution Act which declared New Zealand a self-governing colony and elections were held for the governing assembly a year later.

Initially, voting was restricted to male British subjects, aged at least 21 who owned land worth at least £50, or who paid annual rents of at least £10 for farmland or a city house, or £5 for a rural house. Those serving criminal sentences for treason, felonies or for other serious offences were excluded.

Though Maori men were theoretically entitled to vote, many were unable because the electoral rules excluded communally-held land from counting towards the property qualification, and many Maori followed their traditional customs of sharing land ownership.

Many settlers feared Maori would have the numbers to out-vote Europeans but most Maori saw the 'settler parliament' as having little relevance to them.

As settlement progressed, the capital was shifted to Wellington in 1865 to provide a more central base.

That year, Parliament passed the Native Rights Act which created four Maori electorate seats in the House.

All seats of the House were, and most still are, awarded by winning most votes in a geographical area. A Representation Commission of appointed officials draws the electorate boundaries based on population.

Until 1890, parliament consisted of a range of independent members, overseen by a Legislative Council appointed by the Governor General, on the advice of the Prime Minister.

The length of terms between elections varied, with parliament dissolved whenever it failed to reach agreement. Thus the terms of the first eight parliaments were: two years, five years, five years, four years, four years, two years, three years and three years again. In 1890, Parliament voted for a three-year term and independents made up the chamber for the next three terms.

Early leaders were all English-born, educated and seen to be members of the British upper classes.

The leader of the country was at first called Colonial Secretary or First Minister. This had been formally changed in 1869 to Premier but in 1901 it was informally changed to Prime Minister by Richard Seddon during his term in office.

Seddon, known as King Dick, was the first non-aristocrat to serve as leader. He remains the longest-serving Prime Minister of New Zealand, being in power from 1893 to 1906, when he died in office.

During his term, groups of MPs formed various political parties so they could pursue ideologically-based legislation. This led to the system known as First Past the Post in which the party that won the most seats would form a government.

Seddon joined the Liberal Party, taking over from its

founder John Balance, who had preceded him as premier. Labelled as an 'enemy of elitism', Seddon pushed for Maori and workers' rights but shunned women's suffrage until it became clear he would lose power unless he relented.

Women voted for the first time in the 1893 general election making New Zealand the first country in the world where women could vote (though women were not eligible to stand as candidates until 1919).

Richard Sedden

Seddon was the first leader to espouse the ideals of a welfare state, introducing an old age pension in 1898 and introducing cheap housing schemes.

The country launched a national child welfare programme in 1907.

On September 26, 1907, New Zealand was declared a Dominion, changing its status from a self-governing colony of Britain. As a Dominion, New Zealand became virtually independent, but retained the British monarch as head of state, represented locally by a governor-general appointed in consultation with the New Zealand government.

In 1912, the Reform Party replaced the Liberals in power, led by William Massey (known as Farmer Bill) who was prime minister until he died in office in May 1925. He remains the country's second-longest serving leader.

Massey's nickname came from his backing for the rural sector, which was booming, and Massey University is named after him as it began as an agricultural college.

In 1923, New Zealand was granted the right to carry on its

own international trade negotiations independently of Britain.

The first trade treaty signed by New Zealand was with Japan in 1928.

The British kept control over constitutional changes, defence and some foreign affairs policies until 1931 when the Statute of Westminster relinquished these requirements.

Elizabeth McCombs. Photo: Archives New Zealand (Creative Commons licence).

Elizabeth McCombs was elected the country's first woman MP in 1933.

The Labour Party won power in 1935, led by Australian-born Michael Joseph Savage, whose background was in unionism in Australia. Savage established the social security network to support the unemployed, the sick and the elderly, and in 1938 introduced family benefit payments, health insurance, a minimum wage and a 40-hour week.

Savage's housing minister, John A. Lee, was responsible for the building of the first State houses, built and owned by the State but leased at cheap rates to those on low incomes.

The two politicians fell out and Lee was expelled from the party.

Savage led the country out of the Great Depression of the 1930s and into World War Two.

He forged an alliance with the Maori Christian-based religion the Ratana Church which endures to this day.

Savage, who died in office in 1940 from cancer of the colon, was replaced by Peter Fraser who served for nine years before Labour lost power to the National Party.

Until 1945, rural electorates had often consisted of fewer voters than those in towns and cities. The Labour government changed this to ensure all general electorates consisted of similar numbers of voters.

New Zealand finally achieved full autonomy from Britain in 1947 when its politicians passed the Statute of Westminster Adoption Act, though the act merely confirmed what had been practice for many years.

New Zealand sovereignty is generally regarded to have been established from 1947 because that's when the country took formal control over its foreign policy and the attainment of constitutional and plenary powers by its legislative process.

In 1949, National's Sidney Holland became Prime Minister. Within two years, the government was embroiled in what remains the biggest industrial confrontation in New Zealand's history: the 1951 Waterfront Dispute.

At one stage, more than 22,000 waterfront workers (known as wharfies) and other union members were off the job, prompting the government to declare a national state of emergency. The government and employers deemed the workers' actions to be a strike while workers claimed they were locked out of their jobs.

Michael Joseph Savage

Police and workers fought in the streets as the dispute lasted 151 days. The confrontation created divisions between employers and workers, between unions, police and politicians, and contributed to industrial unrest for the next three decades.

Holland was replaced by Keith Holyoake shortly before the 1957 election won by Labour. The following year, finance minister Arnold Nordmeyer delivered what became known as the 'Black Budget' when he significantly increased taxes for beer, tobacco and petrol.

After one term with Walter Nash as Prime Minister, Holyoake led the Nats back to power in 1960.

In 1961, capital punishment was abolished, except for treason (that remained a capital crime until 1989). The last person legally executed was hanged for murder in 1957. He was the 85th person executed since the first in 1842.

In 1965, the Cook Islands (which had been part of New Zealand since 1900) moved to self-government though their people retained their rights to New Zealand citizenship.

In 1972, Norman Kirk's Labour Party was elected for a single term, with Kirk dying after only 21 months in charge. During his brief leadership, Kirk's cabinet opposed nuclear testing in the Pacific, pronounced February 6 as Waitangi Day (a public holiday to celebrate the country's nationhood) and established the Waitangi Tribunal to settle Maori land and resource claims.

In 1975, National returned to the government benches with Robert Muldoon as Prime Minister. The country was feeling the economic impact of Britain joining the European Community and from global increases in oil prices when they doubled in a year, and doubled again before 1980.

Muldoon's government initiated price and wage freezes and launched a range of energy-related projects under the banner of Think Big. These included expansion of the oil refinery at Marsden Point in Northland, construction of an ironsand processing mill to make steel at Glenbrook in South Auckland, a urea and methanol plant at Taranaki, the Clyde Dam in Central Otago and the Tiwai aluminium smelter at Bluff at the foot of the South Island.

Rising international debt and easing energy prices led to

criticism of the Think Big strategy and National was replaced in 1984 by David Lange's Labour Party.

Labour embarked on the most wide-ranging economic reforms in the country's history.

Under finance minister Roger Douglas, import duties were dropped and a universal Goods and Services Tax (GST) was introduced in October 1986. (It was initially a 10% tax but increased to 12.5% in 1989 and to 15% in 2010.)

Under Labour, industries were deregulated and some state-owned businesses were sold to the private sector to generate funds to settle debt and to encourage competition.

The House of Representatives passed the Constitution Act 1986 (which took effect from January 1, 1987), in which New Zealand 'unilaterally revoked all residual United Kingdom legislative power.' This confirmed New Zealand's status as a free-standing constitutional monarchy whose parliament has unlimited sovereign power.

Lange's government banned nuclear armed warships from New Zealand waters which sparked a diplomatic stand-off with the United States and a suspension of the defence alliance known as the ANZUS treaty. The government also opposed nuclear testing by the French in the South Pacific, and New Zealanders gave wide support to protestors who planned to sail with the Greenpeace vessel *Rainbow Warrior* to demonstrate against underground testing at the Mururoa Atoll, in French Polynesia.

On July 10, 1985, French secret agents bombed and crippled the *Rainbow Warrior* at its berth in Auckland, killing a Portugese photographer aboard. Two agents were charged with murder and other offences but in a plea bargain, they accepted manslaughter convictions and were sentenced to 10 years jail. They served two years before being repatriated to France.

A flotilla of New Zealand yachts still sailed for Mururoa

and eventually the French halted their nuclear testing programme, though they held another series of tests in 1995.

Labour established a Royal Commission of Inquiry into the country's electoral system. In 1986, after much deliberation, it suggested a referendum to offer change, putting forward four models of proportional representation.

Desire for change followed general elections where the party which won most seats was sometimes not the party which secured the most votes overall.

Smaller parties felt disenfranchised; in 1978, the Social Credit Party won 16% of the vote but won just one seat in the House and in 1981 it gained 21% of the vote but took only two seats of 92.

In 1990, New Zealand adopted a Bill of Rights, an act of parliament setting out rights and freedoms to be enjoyed by citizens.

National resumed power in 1990, led by Jim Bolger, and in 1992 a non-binding referendum was held to test whether voters wanted to retain the First Past the Post system, or adopt a proportional representation system based on electoral systems overseas. In the poll, 55% of eligible voters indicated their preference and 84.5% wanted change.

In 1993, at the same time as the general election, a binding referendum was held to decide the new system and 53.4% of voters chose the Mixed Member Proportional (MMP) system.

Under the new system, electors could vote for their preferred candidate in their electorate but also vote for the party they wanted. Any party that gained 5% of the total vote was guaranteed a seat and the number of party seats would be

The Rainbow Warrior.
Photo: Klearchos
Kapoutsis (Creative
Commons licence).

relative to the percentage of votes received and would be filled by candidates named on a party list.

If a candidate won his or her electorate seat, they would take that seat and be ruled off the party list with the next person on that list moving up the rankings.

In 1996, in the first MMP election, the National Party formed a government with the help of Winston Peters' New Zealand First Party. The number of parliamentary seats increased under the new system from 99 to 120. New Zealand First had won 13% of the vote and 17 seats, including all five Maori seats.

A year later, Bolger was replaced by Jenny Shipley who became the country's first woman prime minister. Her appointment was the first of a number of high profile roles filled by women over the next decade, when almost a third of MPs were female.

During that period, women took key constitutional roles such as governor general, speaker of the House of Representatives and chief justice.

After two years in power, Shipley's government was defeated by Labour who formed a coalition with Jim Anderton's Alliance and with support from the Green Party.

The new prime minister was Helen Clark who remained in office for almost nine years. During her term, the country adopted social policies seen to be quite liberal including the legalising of prostitution in 2003 and acceptance of same-sex unions in 2004. After leaving New Zealand politics, Clark was appointed Administrator of the United Nations Development programme, the third-highest position in the UN, in 2009, and in 2016 she announced she would seek the role of Secretary-General of the UN.

John Key and Helen Clark

National returned to power in 2008. Businessman John Key became the country's 38th prime minister and leader of its 49th government when National returned to power in 2008, with support from minority parties ACT, United Future and the Maori Party. General elections in 2011 and 2014 ensured Key and National remained in power after signing confidence and supply agreements with its three minority party partners.

After 40 years of debate about New Zealand's flag, the Key government announced two referenda would be held in 2015 and 2016 to give the public chance to decide whether the nation would change its flag, a Blue Ensign with the Union Flag and four red stars symbolising the Southern Cross. The traditional flag had been in use since 1869 and given statutory recognition in 1902.

In 2015, New Zealanders voted for their favoured alternative to the traditional flag and a second referendum in March 2016 asked New Zealanders to choose between the current flag and the favoured alternative. Only six of 71 electorates voted for change with 56.7% of voters remaining loyal to the current flag.

The New Zealand flag used since 1869

The alternative flag rejected in 2016

In December 2016, Key resigned after eight years at the helm and was replaced as Prime Minister by his finance minister, Bill English.

In November 2017, Jacinda Ardern became New Zealand's 40th Prime Minister (and, at 37, the world's youngest female leader of government) when her Labour Party formed a minority coalition government with New Zealand First, supported by the Greens.

On June 21, 2018, she became only the second elected head of government in the world to give birth while in office, becoming the mother of daughter Neve.

In September 2020, the Ardern-led Labour Party won a majority of seats in a general election, enabling her to form a government without a coalition partner.

Parliament implements new laws for New Zealand through a system in which proposed legislation is usually introduced to the House of Representatives by the ruling party, though it can be proposed by any individual member, in the form of a bill.

The bill is read to the House and debated after which a

vote is taken. Each bill must pass three such votes to be entered into law; if defeated at any stage it is thrown out, though amendments can be made and the bill re-introduced.

Common practice is for most bills to be referred to a select committee made up of parliamentarians from different parties deemed to have expertise in particular areas.

The committee hears submissions from those directly affected by the proposed law change and the general public, and then advises parliament and its law drafters of any need for change identified through the select committee process.

Then the bill goes back to the House for its second and third readings and votes. If passed it is signed off by the governor general, which these days is regarded as a formality.

MPs usually vote in groups according to their party policy but 'votes of conscience' are sometimes allowed in areas of social reform.

Post-2000 examples were changes to laws relating to end of life choice, homosexuality and prostitution.

Today, the country has universal suffrage — one person, one vote, from the age of 18 years. There is no penalty for not voting.

Chapter Five
CONFLICTS

NEW ZEALANDERS have taken part in many international conflicts. Casualties suffered by New Zealanders in both world wars were proportionately high compared to other countries. Conflicts include:

The Second Boer War (1899–1902)

New Zealand offered support to the British Empire in its war on South African soil over land settlement in the independent Boer republics of Orange Free State and Transvaal.

About 6,500 mounted troops left for South Africa, making this New Zealand's first overseas military campaign. Losses were 71 killed in action, 25 killed in accidents and 133 who died from disease.

World War One (1914–1918)

New Zealand suffered the highest rate of casualties and death per capita of any country involved in the war.

The nation sent more than 100,000 troops and nurses to support Britain's war against Germany, which represented about 10% of the population. Maori and Pacific Islanders served for the first time.

By war's end, 16,697 New Zealanders had been killed and 41,317 wounded, a 58% casualty rate.

More than 500 more died during training to go to war, and more than a thousand others died within five years of the German surrender, from injuries sustained.

New Zealand's first significant action was to capture German Samoa where 80 Germans and a gunboat were stationed. A contingent of 1,374 New Zealand soldiers took Samoa without resistance in August 1914.

New Zealand troops fought their first major battle alongside Australian soldiers when they landed at Gallipoli, in Turkey, on April 25, 1915.

In the ensuing battle, 2,701 New Zealanders were killed and 4,852 wounded. New Zealanders and Australians commemorate the landing, and the bond created that day between the two nations, with an annual public holiday every April 25, known as Anzac Day.

Troops also fought in the Middle East and France. In the Battle of the Somme, about 5,500 New Zealanders were wounded and 1,560 were killed.

New Zealand's single worst day of the war was October 17, 1917, when more than 2,700 casualties were suffered in the battle for the Belgian town of Passchendaele. With no ground gained in the assault on the enemy, 45 officers and 800 men were either killed or left fatally wounded between enemy lines.

The cruiser *HMS Philomel* became New Zealand's contribution to the war at sea, losing three of its crew while supporting British naval landings.

In June 1917, a German raider laid mines off the New Zealand coast, sinking merchant ships off Farewell Spit and Three Kings Islands.

A week before the end of the war in November 1918, the New Zealand Division liberated the French town of Le

Quesnoy which had been occupied by the Germans since August 1914. It was the New Zealanders' last significant action in the war.

To this day, the people of Le Quesnoy commemorate the part New Zealand played in its history with a memorial, streets named after places in New Zealand and a primary school named after a Kiwi soldier.

The capture of Le Quesnoy was one of many campaigns on the Western Front, the line that stretched across northern France and Belgium, that claimed the lives of about 12,000 New Zealanders between 1916 and 1918.

World War Two (1939-1945)

Prime Minister Michael Savage declared war on Germany immediately after Britain in September 1939.

In a radio broadcast to the nation, he said:

> 'With gratitude for the past and confidence in the future we range ourselves without fear beside Britain. Where she goes, we go; where she stands, we stand. We are only a small and young nation, but we march with a union of hearts and souls to a common destiny.'

About 140,000 New Zealanders served in the war, with 104,000 in the 2nd New Zealand Expeditionary Force which under Major-General Bernard Freyberg saw active service in Greece, Crete, North Africa, Italy and Yugoslavia.

Almost 9% of the population were engaged and the country suffered almost 12,000 fatalities, the highest death rate per capita of all Commonwealth countries involved in the war.

More than 100,000 men stayed in New Zealand to form the Home Guard.

Other New Zealanders served with the Royal Air Force and the Royal Navy while the country's own naval resources were placed at the command of the British Admiralty. In 1941, the Royal New Zealand Navy was formed.

The country depended on the British Royal Navy and the United States to protect it from the threat of Japanese invasion, after Japan entered the war in December 1941.

German and Japanese surface raiders and submarines ventured into New Zealand waters on a number of missions between 1940 and 1945, sinking four ships.

New Zealanders played a key role in the air, providing more than 10,000 aircrew to the Royal Air Force. Of these, 3,290 were killed while 580 were captured. New Zealander Air Vice Marshal Sir Keith Park famously led the No. 11 Group, Fighter Command, in the Battle of Britain. More than 8,000 New Zealanders were taken prisoner during the war.

Unlike during the Boer War when Maori were not allowed to enlist, nearly 16,000 Maori served during World War Two and the 28th (Maori) Battalion became one of the most decorated units in the New Zealand forces. The pinnacle of recognition was the Victoria Cross won by Te Moananui–a–Kiwa Ngarimu in 1943.

In all, 194,000 men (67% of those aged 18–45) and 10,000 women served in the armed forces here and abroad.

During the war, the country committed about 30% of its national income to the war effort, with the figure reaching 50% between 1942 and 1944.

Malaya (1948–1960)

About 1,300 New Zealanders served in the Malayan Emergency declared by Britain to initially fight guerrillas of the Malayan Races Liberation Army and later to deter communist aggression in South–East Asia.

Fifteen New Zealanders died in Malaya, three of them killed by enemy action.

Korean War (1950–1953)

About 5,000 New Zealand soldiers and sailors served in Korea as part of the forces of the UN Command, led by the United States, following North Korea's invasion of South Korea in 1950. Six frigates and a few smaller craft were sent and they took part in the Battle of Inchon.

New Zealand suffered 112 casualties in Korea, of whom 33 died.

Many troops were deployed in Korea for four years after the war in a peacekeeping role.

The Korean conflict was instrumental in the formation of the ANZUS Treaty in 1951 between the United States, Australia and New Zealand, a defence agreement that remained in place until New Zealand banned entry of nuclear powered or nuclear armed ships into its waters in 1984.

Malaysia (1964-1966)

New Zealand initially declined to support Britain's call for military support in its dispute with Indonesia over its attempts to form the Federation of Malaysia. Prime Minister Keith Holyoake was anxious not to fall out with Indonesia. But when Indonesian paratroopers landed in Johore in September 1964, the New Zealand government authorised its troops already in the region to help hunt them down.

Vietnam War (1964-1975)

This was the first time New Zealand had taken part in a major conflict not involving the United Kingdom. Instead, as part of its commitment to the ANZUS Treaty, New Zealand supplied about 3,500 non-active engineers and military personnel to serve in South Vietnam between mid-1964 and December 1972.

The New Zealand force numbered 543 troops at its peak in 1968, while opposition to their involvement started to grow and protestors took to New Zealand streets, urging the government to withdraw.

By the time the third Labour government ended New

Zealand's involvement, 37 personnel had died on active service and 187 more suffered wounds.

Middle East (1982–ongoing)

New Zealand has helped the United States and the United Kingdom in the Middle East but has generally provided non-combative support. During the Iran–Iraq War in the 1980s, two New Zealand frigates helped monitor merchant shipping in the Persian Gulf, while in 1991, the country supplied three transport aircraft and a medical team to help coalition forces in the Gulf War.

In recent years, New Zealand's most significant military involvement has been in Afghanistan where members of the elite SAS were sent after the September 11, 2001, terrorist attacks on the United States.

In March 2002, they took part in Operation Anaconda against more than 500 Al-Qaeda and Taliban forces.

In 2007, Corporal Willie Apiata was awarded the New Zealand Victoria Cross for bravery after carrying a badly wounded comrade across a battlefield while under fire.

Peacekeeping

New Zealand forces have taken part in many peace-keeping and international observer roles, including Somalia (1992–1994), Bosnia and Herzegovina (1992–2004), Haiti (1994–1995) and Kosovo (1999–2008).

Almost 4,000 New Zealanders have served in East Timor, helping keep the peace there between 1999 and 2003, and in 2006. Four were killed.

Though New Zealand's government opposed the 2003 invasion of Iraq, it agreed to provide a naval frigate and a surveillance aircraft to help the US Command in the Gulf. The country also contributed a small engineering and support force to help reconstruct Iraq after the war.

Compulsory Military Training

Between 1949 and 1959, more than 60,000 young men

were given 18 weeks of compulsory military training. After the scheme was abolished, it was reinstated in 1962 when 3,000 men aged 18 were drawn by ballot to undergo training.

That scheme was scrapped in December 1972. Since then, all military service has been voluntary.

Gallantry

Between 1864 and 1943, 21 New Zealanders were awarded the Imperial Victoria Cross. In 1999, the country instituted the New Zealand Victoria Cross as its premier award for gallantry.

Chapter Six

DEATH AND DISASTERS

THE RELATIVELY small size of New Zealand's population means that disasters have far-reaching effects in the community. It's often said that every household has some connection to every major tragedy.

Significant events have included:

Worst death toll

The largest death toll from any incident in New Zealand's history was the 8,573 who succumbed to the influenza epidemic of 1918.

Globally, more than 500 million were infected and 50 million were killed by the virus, which is believed to have evolved as an avian 'flu which was passed from pigs to humans in much the same way more recent 'bird 'flu' and 'H1N1' viruses mutated.

The virus was present in New Zealand for just three months, from October to December 1918.

Medical experts advised the cancellation of public events and the closure of hotels, billiard halls and other places where large groups met.

Streets were disinfected. Bases were set up where people

were given a spray containing zinc sulphate which was believed to prevent infection — in fact it was medically useless.

In homes, sulphur was thrown on open fires in an attempt to fumigate the house.

Other remedies included a daily dose of quinine, or a teaspoon of sugar with a drop of kerosene. Lemon juice was supposed to be a preventive tonic and shops ran out of lemons.

Some communities were hardly touched, while others were devastated. Auckland city was hard hit, with medical workers unable to keep up with demand.

Bodies were carted in their hundreds by train to the suburb of Glen Eden, where they were laid out under trees awaiting burial because coffins could not be constructed quickly enough.

Studies since have traced the cause and effects of the epidemic and determined that the virus prompted an over-reaction of the body's immune system, thus explaining why most of those killed were young adults to middle-age, rather than the very young or the elderly, who have weaker immune systems.

In the aftermath, the government passed the 1920 Health Act which put in place procedures for dealing with similar events, systems that remained in force until a revamp in 1956.

In 2020, New Zealand introduced a four-level alert system to combat the COVID-19 pandemic sweeping the world.

The country recorded its first confirmed case of the coronavirus on February 28, 2020.

Prime Minister Jacinda Ardern led a plan to control the spread of the virus by closing borders, banning mass gatherings, suspending non-essential businesses with public-facing activities and encouraging physical distancing.

Visitors to New Zealand were required to enter a process of managed isolation and quarantine for 14 days.

By January 4, 2021, the Ministry of Health had recorded 1,825 confirmed and 356 probable cases, with 25 deaths.

By December 2021, a national campaign to encourage vaccinations achieved its target of 90% uptake for all those eligible (aged 12+). A vaccination programme for children aged 5-11 was planned for 2022.

By January 10, 2022, the Ministry of Health had recorded 14,358 confirmed and 375 probable cases of COVID-19 since the first recorded case in February 2020.

There had been 51 deaths from the disease in the same period.

Natural disasters

In terms of loss of life, the worst natural disaster in New Zealand's history was the Napier earthquake of 1931 in which 256 people lost their lives and much of the city was flattened.

The quake began at 10.47am on Tuesday, February 3, and it continued for two and a half minutes. Thousands were injured, and more than 400 were hospitalised.

Locals had noticed strange conditions beforehand — oppressive heat and humidity, still air and a sea that changed suddenly from flat calm to throwing huge waves onto beaches.

Birds were absent and other animals showed unusual signs of restlessness. For years afterwards, survivors talked of 'earthquake weather'.

Minutes after the quake, fire broke out in a main street Napier chemist shop and quickly spread through the centre of town. People trapped in rubble were burnt alive. Fire fighters had no means to tackle the blazes as water pipes had been broken.

The navy ship *HMS Veronica* was fortunately in port and its sailors provided immediate assistance in rescues. *HMS*

Diomede and *HMS Dunedin* were despatched from Auckland with medical personnel and supplies, food and tents, as well as sailors to maintain order and prevent looting.

Napier's Post Office during the 1931 earthquake. Photo: Archives New Zealand (Creative Commons licence).

Almost all of Napier's buildings and much of Hastings was destroyed. The Ahuriri Lagoon on which locals used to sail small yachts was lifted more than two metres and dried out completely. It is now the site of the Hawkes Bay airport.

Napier's port after the 1931 earthquake. Photo: Archives New Zealand (Creative Commons Licence).

More than 40 square kilometres of seabed was turned into dry land along Napier's coastline, much of it now used by industry.

Scientists determined the quake was centred 15km north of Napier at a depth of 20km.

It measured 7.8 on the Richter scale.

During the Great Depression of the 1930s, workers rebuilt the cities, with Napier's new buildings designed in the art deco fashion of the time.

Today, Napier's architecture is a major tourism draw. No building in either Napier or Hastings has been built higher than five storeys.

New Zealand suffered another major earthquake disaster on February 22, 2011, when 185 people died with most crushed to death or killed by falling debris in Christchurch. More than 6,500 were treated for minor injuries and hundreds more for serious injuries.

The quake measured 6.3 on the Richter scale. The lunchtime quake did most damage to the central business district where workers and tourists were trapped in buildings as they collapsed. Rescuers managed to pull 74 survivors from the rubble.

More than half of the fatalities occurred in the CTV (Canterbury Television) building when it collapsed. It housed a foreign language school and a childcare centre as well as the local television station studios.

Other large buildings destroyed included the six-storey Pyne Gould Corporation building, in which 18 died, and the Grand Chancellor Hotel which had to be demolished when the quake left it on a dangerous lean.

Historic buildings including the iconic Christchurch Cathedral, the Arts Centre and the Council Chambers were seriously damaged.

The Government committed to rebuilding these historic

places but more than 800 commercial buildings were written off.

An estimated 100,000 homes were damaged of which at least 10,000 faced demolition.

Seismologists said the shake was an aftershock of the 7.1 scale earthquake that hit the city the previous September when no one was harmed. The February quake was more damaging because it was centred only 10km from the CBD and at a depth of only 5km, meaning it was closer to the city and closer to the earth's surface.

The initial earthquake was centred at Darfield 40km inland from Christchurch at a depth of 10kms, on a previously unidentified fault running out from the Alpine Fault which cuts down the Southern Alps.

Christchurch after the 2011 earthquake. Photo: New Zealand Defence Forces (Creative Commons licence).

One of the biggest problems for home owners was liquefaction — a wet winter had pushed the water table up towards the surface and when the earthquake hit larger gravels and silts sunk, while water and fine sands rose, turning the ground to an unstable sludge. Sewer, power and communications lines were destroyed.

Following the September quake, Canterbury experienced thousands of aftershocks.

Early estimates indicated the September quake would cost insurers at least $4 billion while the cost of the February quake would exceed $16 billion. In April 2013, the Government forecast it would cost up to $40 billion to rebuild the city. Such was the enormity of the financial impact, the government had to bail out insurance company AMI with a $500 million financial guarantee.

A Royal Commission investigated building-related issues in the earthquake and found the the Christchurch City Council should not have granted a building permit for the CTV building.

Disruption to Christchurch continued for years after the 2011 earthquake. Photo: Andy Miah (Creative Commons licence).

In 1929, 17 people were killed by an earthquake measuring 7.8 on the Richter scale that struck the Buller Gorge, triggering major landslides. Buildings were badly damaged in Greymouth, Westport and Nelson. The local landscape was changed significantly, not least by the creation of 38 new lakes.

In 1968, a 7.1 scale earthquake destroyed the town of Inangahua near Reefton in the South Island. Though 70% of the town's buildings came down, only three people were killed. Many more would have died had the area not been so sparsely populated.

In November 2016, a 7.8 scale earthquake near Kaikoura caused two deaths and severely damaged property, roads and bridges in the area. The earthquake caused significant damages to buildings in Wellington, forcing some to be demolished.

More than 100 people died when Mt Tarawera erupted on June 10, 1886, throwing molten scoria down its sides and billowing a cloud of ash an estimated 10kms into the sky. The eruption, near Rotorua, was heard by residents in the South Island and earth tremors could be felt throughout the North Island.

The settlements of Te Tapahoro, Moura, Te Ariki, Totarariki and Waingongogongo were destroyed or buried beneath mud and ash as land around the mountain was devastated. The world famous Pink and White Terraces, a rock formation tinted by hot mineral waters, were destroyed by the eruption, creating a 100-metre deep crater which later filled to form Lake Rotomahana, 10 times larger than the original lake.

The official death toll was 150, though research since suggests the actual toll was no more than 120.

On December 9, 2019, the volcanic island Whakaari/White Island erupted, killing 21 and injuring 26, most of whom suffered severe burns. Of the 47 people who were on the island at the time of the eruption, 38 were passengers from the *Ovation of the Seas* cruise ship that had berthed at Tauranga that day.

The death toll included citizens of Australia (14), United States (5) and New Zealand (2); those injured came from Australia (10), United States (4), Germany (4), New Zealand (3), United Kingdom (2), China (2) and Malaysia (1).

WorkSafe New Zealand and police launched an investigation into the circumstances of the disaster. In April 2020, legal action was started against the Royal Caribbean cruise line by relatives of the victims.

Rail disasters

New Zealand's worst rail disaster took place on Christmas Eve, 1953 with 151 passengers killed when the Tangiwai rail bridge collapsed beneath the Wellington to Auckland overnight express. The train was full, with 11 carriages carrying 285 passengers north for the festive season.

It was late at night and pitch-black when the train approached the Whangaehu River bridge, between Waiouru and Ohakune. Minutes earlier, a lahar or volcanic flood had washed down the Whangaehu Glacier on Mt Ruapehu. A wall of ash that had long dammed the mountain's crater lake had collapsed, sending a tidal wave of water carrying huge boulders into the river where it took out the centre span of the rail bridge, leaving the tracks still connected but swinging in the wind. No warning system was in place and the train driver was unaware of the danger as the express carried on northwards.

The steam locomotive lurched across the river, its momentum carrying it and the first carriage to the other side. The next five carriages carrying passengers in second class broke free and careered into the swollen river. Carriage six was the most forward of the first class carriages. It teetered on the brink of the drop, then fell in.

Of the 176 second class passengers, only 28 survived.

The army was sent from Waiouru to help in the rescue and the recovery of bodies, many of which were washed several kilometres downstream.

One carriage was carried nearly 5km. Twenty bodies were never officially recovered but for years afterwards, farmers reported finding skeletal remains on the riverbank.

New Zealand's second worst rail disaster occurred on June 4, 1943, near Hyde, Central Otago. Of 113 passengers, 21 were killed and 47 were injured.

Maritime disasters

New Zealand's worst maritime disaster was the grounding of the naval steam-sailship *HMS Orpheus* on the Manukau Harbour bar in 1863, with the loss of 189 lives from the 259 aboard.

The near-new Royal Navy ship was an early combination of sail and steam-driven engine and was sent to New Zealand at the height of the Maori Land Wars loaded with troops, field supplies and ammunition to reinforce the British positions.

After a string of captaincy errors which included following an old chart, taking the wrong course through the treacherous bar crossing area and ignoring the frantic semaphore (hoisted flags) signalling from the land, she grounded on a sandbank. Three separate inquiries tried to lay blame on the Manukau signalman Thomas Wing and his then 18-year-old son who was assisting him.

But eventually the truth came out — a navy deserter who had been recaptured in Sydney was the only man to have crossed the bar before but when he warned the captain they were taking a bad course he was ignored. Wing also saw the ship heading too far south and initially signalled *Orpheus* by flag that she should head north, later changing that to 'Stop, do not take the bar.' His instructions were ignored by the master Commodore W.F. Burnett.

The country's early history involved many shipwrecks that led to multiple deaths.

The *Fiery Star* went down off the Chatham Islands in May 1865 with the loss of all 79 aboard; in 1881, the *SS Tararua* was lost off Waipapa Point in the Caitlins and 131 were killed; in 1886, the *General Grant* went down off the Auckland Islands with the loss of 68 lives and a cargo of gold bullion, which remains the subject of salvage interest to this day; in October 1894, the *SS Wairarapa* hit rocks near Great Barrier Island and 121 died; and in 1909, the *SS Penguin* was shipwrecked off Cape Terawhiti and 75 people died.

The worst marine disaster of the past 100 years was the sinking of the inter-island ferry *Wahine* inside Wellington Harbour in the early morning of April 4, 1968.

The ship carried 610 passengers including 41 children, and

123 crew. When the ferry grounded, and the passengers and crew were forced to abandon ship, 51 people perished and two died later from their injuries.

The ferry entered the harbour during the worst storm recorded in New Zealand, when winds of up to 275 km/h ripped the roofs from more than 90 Wellington houses.

The captain tried to turn back to sea but the ship was thrown onto Barrett Reef. At 7.02am, the ship issued an SOS.

After almost six hours anchored on the reef after being beached, the sea pushed *Wahine* violently to starboard and the order was given to prepare to abandon ship. Rescuers using all manner of craft from rubber inflatables to jet boats, surf boats and yachts worked with Harbour Board tugs and official emergency services in a bid to save lives. Their efforts prevented greater loss of life.

In 1985, the Greenpeace protest ship *Rainbow Warrior* was sunk at its berth in Auckland by two bombs planted by French secret service agents, two of whom were captured and convicted of manslaughter. A Portuguese photographer was killed in the explosion.

Aviation disasters

The country's deadliest peacetime accident occurred on November 28, 1979, when Air New Zealand flight TE901, a sightseeing trip over the Antarctic ice, crashed into Mt Erebus. The flight's 237 passengers and 20 crew were killed.

The incident resonates in the country's history to this day — it is often said that everyone in New Zealand knew someone who was on the flight.

An inquiry into the crash resulted in a statement by Justice Peter Mahon that company executives had presented 'an orchestrated litany of lies' and although appeals to the Privy Council led to that aspect being dismissed, controversy still surrounds the case.

It was the airline's 14th scenic flight to the frozen continent but the first for pilot Jim Collins and co-pilot Greg Cassin. Mountaineer Sir Edmund Hillary was to have been the guide but was forced to withdraw the day before, his place taken by his friend Peter Mulgrew. Passengers paid $359 each for the trip.

The McDonnell Douglas DC10 took off from Christchurch at 8am and was to have returned by 7pm. The alarm was raised after 9pm, by which time the company knew the plane could no longer be in the air as it would have run out of fuel.

A search was initiated by the United States Navy aircraft based at McMurdo Sound and they spotted wreckage at midnight but it was 9am next day before helicopters could land and confirm the outcome.

The task of recovering the bodies of the deceased was long, involved and grisly. New Zealand police and forensic scientists had to dig bodies from beneath the wreckage of the fuselage, photograph and tag every piece of remains and these were then sent back to the mainland for identification.

The dead included 180 New Zealanders, 24 Japanese, 22 Americans, six from the United Kingdom and one each from Australia, Switzerland and France.

The initial inquiry by New Zealand's Air Accident Inspector blamed pilot error.

The public did not accept this and the government instituted a full hearing before Justice Mahon, but then baulked at his findings which showed that the airline had altered the flight path set into the plane's instruments the day before take-off but had not informed the crew.

In 2008, 29 years to the day after the Erebus disaster, an Air New Zealand A320 Airbus crashed off the coast of France, killing seven. On September 10, 2010, nine people were killed when a Walter Fletcher FU-24 crashed soon after taking off from the Fox Glacier airstrip.

Mining disasters

Rich coal seams were discovered on the west coast of the South Island in the mid-1880s and have since been the basis of the region's economy, but not without multiple tragedies generally due to build-up of methane, or 'fire damp', and resultant explosions underground when it is ignited.

The state-owned Strongman Mine near Brunner had been in production for several years when an explosion ripped through it on March 25, 1896.

Of the 240 men at work, 65 were killed by the blast or the oxygen deprivation and creation of carbon monoxide that followed it.

Miners came from all around the coast to aid in the recovery of bodies and eventually all were brought out, many rescuers falling unconscious during the operation and having to be carried out.

In 1939, the government opened a mine at Rununga and it operated without trouble until 1967, when 19 men were killed by a similar event.

On the morning of September 12, 1914, an explosion rocked through Ralph's Mine in the centre of Huntly, killing 43 of the 60 men at work.

The blast was sparked by the open flame of one miner's acetylene cap light.

A similar tragedy occurred on the afternoon of November 19, 2010, when a methane blast ripped through the Pike River coal mine near Greymouth. Of the 31 men working underground, 29 were killed. The victims had been working about 1,500 metres inside from the mine entrance which burrowed horizontally beneath a mountain range. Two men escaped the initial blast.

As rescuers gathered and prepared to enter the mine for a

recovery operation, a second blast occurred on November 24 and a third explosion on November 26.

These prompted all rescue and body recovery attempts to be called off and the mine entrance was sealed.

The company that owned the mine was soon placed in receivership, ending plans to export around $200 million in high grade coal to China and India annually.

Fire disasters

New Zealand's worst fire disaster occurred on the afternoon of November 18, 1947, when the rambling Ballantyne's Department Store on the corner of Colombo and Cashel Streets in central Christchurch went up in flames, causing the deaths of 41 workers.

Smoke was seen coming from a cellar area at 3.30pm and soon after the staff and customers on the ground floor were evacuated.

But there was significant delay in passing the advice to leave to those working on the upper three floors of the store, which was a phalanx of seven individual buildings linked together.

Not all parts of the upper floors had access to fire escapes and when the flames burst from the cellar and windows began to explode from the ground floor out into the street it was already too late for those upstairs in the dressmaking, millinery and accounts departments, many of whom had just returned to work after their tea break. The blaze was not extinguished until 8pm.

An inquiry found too few firefighters were sent to the scene and ladders taken to the site were not long enough to reach the fourth floor to get people out. The store had insufficient fire escapes, no sprinkler system and no company plan for staff and customer evacuation in the event of fire or other emergency.

All of these factors were remedied in the following years

by change to fire regulations for large public buildings.

In 1942, almost 40 people died in a fire at Seacliff Asylum, a psychiatric hospital near Dunedin. The 19th century building was the largest in the country and the fire victims died when they were trapped in a locked ward in a wooden outbuilding.

Construction disaster

A Department of Conservation officer and 13 students from Greymouth's Tai Poutini Polytechnic were killed when a scenic viewing platform in the Paparoa National Park collapsed on April 28, 1995. Known as the Cave Creek Disaster (after a stream in the park), the platform had been built 40 metres above rocks by the Department.

A Commission of Inquiry raised concerns about the construction of the platform and said the root causes of the failure were systemic problems in the department. The Minister of Conservation, Denis Marshall, resigned a year after the accident, having been heavily criticised for his department's role. The department paid $2.6 million to victims' families and inspected more than 500 of its structures throughout the country, closing 65 for repairs.

Terrorism

On March 15, 2019, a lone gunman killed 51 people and injured 49 more in a terrorist attack at the Al Noor Mosque in the Christchurch suburb of Riccarton, followed by an attack at the Linwood Islamic Centre.

Australian Brenton Tarrant (28), an avowed white supremacist, live-streamed the mosque attack on Facebook.

In March 2020, he pleaded guilty to 51 charges of murder, 40 charges of attempt murder and engaging in a terrorist act. In August2020, he was sentenced to life imprisonment without parole.

Prime Minister Jacinda Ardern described the massacre as 'one of New Zealand's darkest days'.

Chapter Seven

PEOPLE

Population

Since 1851, New Zealand has held a regular census to learn about the size and composition of its population. The census, held every three to five years, has only been cancelled three times — in 1931 during the Great Depression, 1941 during World War Two and in 2011 when the disastrous Christchurch earthquake led to about 70,000 residents temporarily fleeing the city shortly before the census was due to be held.

In the latter half of the 19th century, when Europeans began settling in large numbers in New Zealand, urban populations changed rapidly depending where men moved to seek work.

But in 1901, the population of the North Island exceeded that of the South Island for the first time, and has stayed that way since.

By 1906, the total recorded population was 948,649 (of whom 53.7% lived in the North Island), while 5% of the population was Maori. Only 151 divorces were recorded.

The nation reached the one million mark in 1908 and life

expectancy for men was estimated at 59.2 years and for women at 61.7 years.

By 1951, when Maori and those of European descent were given the same census forms for the first time and given equal status, the population was 1.9 million with 67.3% living in the North Island.

A year later, the population topped two million.

By 1971, the population had grown to 2.9 million of whom almost 8% were Maori. Life expectancy had improved by 10 years for men (to 69) and by more than 13 years for women (to 75.4 years) over the past half century. The annual rate of marriage and childbirth was the highest yet recorded. Almost nine in 1,000 people a year were marrying and 36.5 babies were being born for every 1,000 population. Divorces had also increased to 5,400.

In 1973, New Zealand boasted it had three million people — and 60 million sheep.

The ethnic make-up of the population changed markedly in the latter half of the century as unskilled workers were recruited from the Pacific Islands and Asians settled mainly in Auckland.

By 2001, the nation had 3.7 million residents, of whom 14.7% were Maori, 6.5% were Asian and 6.6% were Pacific Islanders.

Most immigration was to Auckland which now had more than a quarter of the country's population within its boundaries.

In 2003, the population reached four million.

In 2011, Statistics New Zealand estimated the population was growing by one person every 10 minutes and 46 seconds.

In March 2020, New Zealand's population exceeded five million for the first time.

Honours

Until 1975, New Zealand recognised its high achievers

through the British honours system. The first knighthood was awarded to Governor George Grey in 1848.

In 1975, two uniquely New Zealand awards were introduced — the Queen's Service Order and its affiliated Medal.

In 1987, the Order of New Zealand was introduced and a decade later, most of the British honours were scrapped in favour of a five-level New Zealand Order of Merit.

In 2009, the government announced the return to British knighthoods with past recipients of the New Zealand Order of Merit being eligible to take them up.

One simple way New Zealand recognises its heroes has been through using their images on banknotes.

$5 note – Sir Edmund Hillary

Chosen by *Time* magazine as one of its 20 'Heroes of the 20th Century', Sir Ed earned his place in world history on May 29, 1953, when he and Tenzing Norgay of Nepal became the first climbers to conquer Mt Everest's 29,028 feet (8,850 metres) summit and stand on the highest place on earth. Born in 1920, Sir Ed led the life of an adventurer with expeditions to places like the Antarctic and the Ganges but his greatest passion was his humanitarian work with the Sherpa people of the Himalayas. When he died in 2008, he became the first private citizen to be given a State funeral.

$10 note — Kate Sheppard

She is widely regarded as the leader of the suffrage movement in New Zealand, the first country in the world to give women the vote. Born in 1847, she grew up in Liverpool, England, but emigrated to New Zealand at 22.

She led the Women's Christian Temperance Union and was the president of the National Council of Women. She died in 1930.

$50 note — Sir Apirana Ngata

Born in 1874, he played a significant role in the revival of Maori people and culture after Maori population had fallen

Kate Sheppard. Photo: Archives New Zealand (Creative Commons licence).

from about 100,000 in 1840 to 40,000 by the end of the 19th century.

He was the first Maori to graduate from a New Zealand university (with a law degree) becoming a respected Maori leader and an elected Member of Parliament for 38 years.

At the start of World War Two, he urged Maori to enlist, saying it was their 'price of citizenship'.

$100 note — Baron Ernest Rutherford

Widely acclaimed as the father of modern atomic physics, Rutherford was awarded the Nobel Prize in Chemistry in 1908 and became a baron in 1931. He is widely credited with being the first scientist to split the atom.

In 1899, he coined the terms alpha and beta as scientific terms to differentiate between two types of radioactivity. He died in Britain in 1937, aged 66.

War heroes

New Zealand has had many heroes, acclaimed for their bravery. These include:

Nancy Wake, resistance fighter

Wellington-born Nancy Wake was the most decorated servicewoman of World War Two after leading 7,000 members of the French resistance in the battle to overcome the Nazi occupiers.

She was married to a wealthy French businessman executed by the Gestapo after he refused to reveal her whereabouts. The Gestapo code-named her the 'White Mouse' and offered a five-million franc bounty for her capture when she headed their most-wanted list. She retired to the UK to live her old age in relative anonymity but in 2004 was awarded the Companion of the Order of Australia and the New

Zealand Returned Services Association's highest honour, the RSA Badge in Gold, as well as life membership.

Sir Keith Park, Battle of Britain leader

Sir Keith was the commander of the RAF during the Battle of Britain in World War Two, about whom Lord Tedder (chief of the RAF) said in 1947: 'If any one man won the Battle of Britain, he did.' Born in Thames, and educated in Dunedin, Keith Park served with the Royal Artillery in France during World War One before a wound led to his transfer to the air corps. He became a decorated fighter pilot and went on to lead the RAF.

Charles Upham, dual Victoria Cross winner

Charles Upham. Photo: Archives New Zealand (Creative Commons licence).

This Canterbury farmer joined the New Zealand troops shipped to Egypt in December 1939 and became the only soldier ever to be nominated for three Victoria Crosses. His bravery in various World War Two battles led to him being awarded two VCs, the only front-line soldier to receive such an honour, and one of only three men to get the award twice (the others were medics).

Science and medicine

New Zealanders have made an important contribution to the world of science and medicine. They include:

William Pickering

Born in Havelock, Marlborough, Dr Pickering left New Zealand as a young scientist and became a central figure in the 'space race'.

In 1958, as director of NASA's Jet Propulsion Laboratory, he led the project to launch the first United States satellite, Explorer 1, into Earth's orbit. He was awarded NASA's Distinguished Service Medal, the US National Medal of

Science and was given an honorary knighthood in 1976. He went to the same primary school as atomic physicist Ernest Rutherford.

Alan McDiarmid

One of three New Zealanders to win a Nobel Prize, McDiarmid was the co-inventor of a range of polymers which have changed the future of electronics. His 2000 Nobel Prize was for the discovery of metallic-like electrical conduction in polymeric materials more usually associated with highly insulating plastics. Born in Masterton, McDiarmid died in Philadelphia aged 79.

Sir Brian Barratt-Boyes

Born in 1924, Sir Brian became one of the world's most eminent heart surgeons, famous for his development of techniques to replace defective heart valves and for finding new ways to treat babies born with heart defects. In the 1950s, he pioneered the development of cardiopulmonary bypass in New Zealand. Despite many opportunities to move overseas, Sir Brian remained with his team at Auckland's Greenlane Hospital. He died in 2006.

Maurice Wilkins

Born in Pongaroa, north Wairarapa, in 1916, Wilkins was a physicist whose meticulous research is credited with the discovery of DNA molecule structure, a discovery regarded as one of the greatest scientific breakthroughs of all time. His work earned him a Nobel Prize for Physics. He died in 2004, aged 87.

The arts

New Zealanders who have been internationally prominent in the arts have included:

Rewi Alley, writer

Born in Springfield, Canterbury, in 1897, Alley went to China in 1927 and spent half a century writing about China and the Communist revolution. He was a key figure in the establishment of industrial co-operatives and technical training schools, and in 1977, the Premier Deng Xiaoping honoured his 80th birthday with a banquet in Beijing. He spent the last years of his life (he died in 1987) venerated as a hero of China.

Sir Peter Jackson, film-maker

Born in 1961, Sir Peter has been New Zealand's most successful film-maker, winning international recognition as a director, producer, actor and screenwriter. He is best known for his *Lord of the Rings* trilogy, which helped earn him three Academy Awards, including award for Best Director in 2003. The second of the trilogy, *Return of the King*, won 11 Oscars. His breakthrough movie was the New Zealand-set *Heavenly Creatures* which earned him an Academy Award Best Screenplay nomination, shared with his partner, Fran Walsh. In 2012, he started another trilogy with *The Hobbit: An Unexpected Journey*.

Dame Jane Campion, film-maker

Born in 1954, Dame Jane became only the second woman to be nominated for an Academy Award for Best Director and she became the first woman to receive the Palme d'Or award for her film *The Piano* (1993). She won a Best Original Screenplay Oscar for *The Piano*.

Since 1980, more than 20 New Zealanders have won Oscars, with many more nominated.

Taika Waititi, film-maker and actor

Born in 1975, Waititi has won multiple awards for his 2019 movie *Jojo Rabbit* (Academy Award, British Academy Film Award and Writers Guild of America Award for Best Adapted Screenplay; Grammy Award for Best Compilation Soundtrack). Other feature films *Boy* (2010) and *Hunt for the Wilderpeople* (2016) have each been New Zealand's top-grossing films.

Dame Kiri Te Kanawa, opera singer

Born in Gisborne in 1944, Dame Kiri is arguably the best soprano of her generation, and her work has been acclaimed around the world. In 1981, she sang Handel's *Let the Bright Seraphim* at the wedding of Prince Charles and Lady Diana Spencer before a television audience estimated at more than half a billion people.

Neil Finn, musician and song-writer

Best known for his work with Split Enz, Crowded House and Fleetwood Mac, the Te Awamutu-raised singer and song-writer has been responsible for more international hits than any other New Zealander with *Don't Dream It's Over* the most-played Kiwi song on radio in the world.

Lorde, singer and song-writer

Born in 1996, Ella Marija Lani Yelich-O'Connor, better known by her stage name Lorde, became the youngest solo artist in nearly 20 years to have a US Billboard No. 1 hit when her song *Royals* became a worldwide success in 2013, winning her two Grammy Awards.

Katherine Mansfield, fiction writer

Born Kathleen Beauchamp in 1888, she wrote highly-acclaimed short stories under her more familiar pen name as she moved to Britain in 1908 and befriended writers such as D.H.Lawrence and Virginia Woolf. She died at 34 but her work remains the subject of much interest and study.

Eleanor Catton, fiction writer

Canadian-born Aucklander Catton won the 2013 Man Booker Prize for her second novel, *The Luminaries*, and became the youngest-ever winner of the award. By mid-2014, the book had reportedly sold 560,000 copies.

Other writers

Other successful New Zealand writers include Keri Hulme (1947–2021), whose only novel *The Bone People* won the 1985 Booker Prize, and Lloyd Jones (1955–) whose *Mister Pip* was short-listed for the 2007 Booker Prize but won the

Commonwealth Writers' Prize. Dame Ngaio Marsh (1895–1982) wrote more than 30 highly-popular detective novels while Janet Frame, the pen name of Nene Janet Paterson Clutha (1924-2004), wrote more than 20 acclaimed novels, and autobiographical and poetry works.

Chapter Eight
INVENTIONS

NEW ZEALAND inventors have a proud record of creating things the rest of the world really needs. Among the most famous Kiwi inventions are:

Referee's whistle

New Zealand referee William Atack became the first person in the world to use a whistle to stop a game of sport in 1884.

Eggbeater

Kiwi Ernest Godward was a serial inventor, coming up with designs for eggbeaters, burglar-proof windows and the world's first spiral hair pin. He sold the patent for the hair pin for US$20,000, a huge amount in 1901.

Flying

Many New Zealanders claim it was a Kiwi who first got an aircraft off the ground. Timaru's Richard Pearse was working on powered flight concepts from 1899 and built his first two-cylinder petrol engine by 1902 for powered flight, and flew it for 150 metres in 1903.

Splitting the atom

Kiwi scientist Baron Ernest Rutherford was the first in

the world to split the atom in 1919. He was awarded a Nobel Prize for his work with radioactivity.

Ernest Rutherford, Nobel Prize winner. Photo: Public domain.

Brewing techniques

Morton W. Coutts revolutionised the brewing of beer by developing the process of continuous fermentation in the 1930s. He was also the first person to broadcast television signals in New Zealand and the first to send a telegraph message to Britain. He died aged 100 in 2004.

Electric fences

An early version of the electric fence was developed by Kiwi inventor William Gallagher in 1937. He used an ignition coil from his car and a Meccano set to make the first electric fence.

Jet boats

Farmer William Hamilton invented the world's first propellerless jet boat in 1953. He also is responsible for inventing the hay lift, an advanced air compressor and a machine that smooths ice on skating rinks.

Disposable syringe

In 1956, Timaru pharmacist Colin Murdoch patented the idea for the disposable syringe, a simple device that has saved millions of lives and helped diabetes sufferers around the world. He also conceived the tranquiliser dart gun for use on animals.

Jogging

Running coach Arthur Lydiard developed a training technique for runners that the world now calls jogging. It helped win Olympic gold medals for his proteges Peter Snell and Murray Halberg at the 1960 Rome Olympics.

Bungy

Daredevil AJ Hackett pioneered the bungy jump, opening

the world's first commercial jump site in 1988, the year after he illegally leapt from the Eiffel Tower in Paris.

Jetpack

Christchurch inventor Glenn Martin developed a jet pack that enables fliers to stay aloft for half an hour. He launched the jetpack at the Oshkosh air show in the United States in July 2008 and his company began taking orders.

Amphibious vehicle

Alan Gibbs invented the world's first high speed sports vehicle that travelled on water as well as land. It was launched to worldwide publicity when Sir Richard Branson drove the Aquada across the Thames river in London and in 2004 set a record in it for crossing the English Channel.

Other novel forms of transport

In recent years, Kiwi inventors have given the world the Blokart (a three-wheeled wind-powered kart), the Schweeb (a man-powered high-speed monorail racer) and the Zorb (a transparent ball that can be powered across the surface of water by occupants walking inside).

Chapter Nine
SPORTS

NEW ZEALAND has a proud sporting history, and has achieved much international success in various sports. The most popular sports include:

Rugby Union

The national sport is rugby union and the national side, known as the All Blacks, has been the world's most successful team over the past century, achieving an 85% winning record.

The first game of rugby was played in New Zealand in Nelson in 1870, when Charles John Monro, the son of the Speaker of the House of Representatives, organised a match, having seen the game played in England. International teams began visiting New Zealand in 1882 and in 1892, the New Zealand Rugby Football Union was formed. A year later, the union picked black shirts for its national side, a decision that would lead to the eventual adoption of All Blacks as the team's nickname.

A New Zealand team first toured Britain in 1905, starting a rivalry that continues today.

In 1981, a tour of New Zealand by the South African national side led to widespread protests and riots as police clashed with those demonstrating against apartheid in the republic.

In 1987, New Zealand hosted and won the inaugural Rugby World Cup and in 1995, the sport turned professional.

In 2011, New Zealand hosted its second Rugby World Cup competition, despite games planned for Christchurch having to be relocated due to the huge earthquake earlier in the year, and won the tournament for the second time.

New Zealand won the William Webb Ellis Cup for the third time in 2015 when it won the final of the Rugby World Cup in England.

Rugby League

The first rugby league match in New Zealand was played in 1908 and the national team, known as The Kiwis, has been among the best-performing in the world since.

New Zealand won rugby league's World Cup in 2008 and were runners-up in 2013. New Zealand's only professional league team is the NZ Warriors who play in the Australasian National Rugby League (NRL) competition.

Football

Association football, or soccer as it's often known in New Zealand, has grown in popularity, especially since the national team (known as the All Whites) first reached the World Cup finals in 1982. The team reached the 2010 finals in South Africa, being undefeated with three draws. The Wellington Phoenix club plays in the professional Australian A-League.

Netball

The most popular sport for women has been netball and New Zealand's national side, the Silver Ferns, has developed a long rivalry with Australia for the title of best team in the world.

Basketball

The Auckland-based New Zealand Breakers play in the

Australian National Basketball League (NBL), a competition they won in 2011, 2012, 2013 and 2015).

Olympic Games

New Zealand has traditionally performed well at summer Olympics, when its medal count is compared on a per capita basis with other countries. Middle distance running provided New Zealand with gold medalists Jack Lovelock (Berlin 1936), Murray Halberg (Rome 1960), Peter Snell (Rome 1960 and Tokyo 1964) and John Walker (Montreal 1976).

Walker became the first man to run a mile in less than 3 min 50 secs when he set a world record at Gothenberg, Sweden, in 1975. Snell had set a world record for the mile in Whanganui in 1962.

Walker Harry Kerr was the first New Zealander to win a medal, a bronze, when he represented Australasia at the 1908 London Games.

The first New Zealander to win a gold medal was swimmer Malcolm Champion in 1912, also representing a combined Australia–New Zealand team.

In 1920, D'Arcy Hadfield won the first medal for a New Zealand–entered team when he came third at a rowing event in Antwerp. Eight years later, at the Amsterdam Games, boxer Ted Morgan landed the country's first gold medal.

Long jumper Yvette Williams became New Zealand's first woman gold medalist at the 1952 Helsinki Games and in 1954 set the world record for her event with a leap of 6.28 metres. In 1987, she was named Athlete of the Century on the 100th anniversary of Athletics New Zealand. She died in April 2019 but was posthumously awarded a Dame Commander of the New Zealand Order of Merit in the Queen's Birthday Honours.

Water sports have produced many Olympic medals for the country, in yachting, kayaking and rowing. Skipper Russell Coutts won gold in the Finn class at the Los Angeles games in 1984 before helping New Zealand win the America's Cup in 1995 and 2000.

New Zealand's most successful Olympian is canoeist Dame Lisa Carrington who won five gold medals and a bronze medal, competing at the 2012, 2016 and 2020 summer Olympics. She was awarded her Dame Companion of the New Zealand Order of Merit for services to canoe racing in 2022.

Motorsport

Motorsport became popular in New Zealand after Bruce McLaren finished second in the world grand prix championship in 1960, and fellow Kiwi Denny Hulme won the title in 1967. Scott Dixon won America's IndyCar title in 2009.

Hugh Anderson won four Grand Prix world road motorcycle racing championships (1963–1965) and Graeme Crosby achieved 10 Grand Prix podium finishes (1980–1982).

The country has produced three winners of the world speedway track title: Ronnie Moore, Barry Briggs and five-time winner Ivan Mauger.

Golf

Three New Zealand golfers have won majors. Left-hander Bob Charles took the 1963 British Open at Royal Lytham and St Annes, and was knighted for his achievements in 1999, and Michael Campbell beat Tiger Woods for the US Open at Pinehurst in 2005.

Korean-born New Zealander Lydia Ko became the youngest woman to win a major championship, winning The Evian Championship in France in 2015 at the age of 18. Earlier that year, she became the youngest golfer of either sex to be ranked No. 1 in the world rankings for professional golf at 17 years 9 months and 8 days of age.

New Zealand's Steve Williams, once the long-time caddy for Tiger Woods, is considered one of the best caddies in the sport.

Cricket

The New Zealand national cricket team played its first test during the 1929–1930 season, against England, but did not win its first game until 25 years later. The team, now known as the Black Caps, has been beaten semi-finalists at six ICC Cricket World Cups and were runners-up at the 2015 World Cup staged in New Zealand and at the 2019 event in the United Kingdom. The team won the inaugural ICC World Test Championship, held between 2019 and 2021, beating India in the final.

Boxing

Timaru blacksmith Bob Fitzsimmons, who emigrated from England as a nine-year-old, became world heavyweight boxing champion in 1896. More than a century later, in November 2000, South Aucklander David Tua attempted to land three world heavyweight titles but was beaten by champion Lennox Lewis. New Zealand boxer Joseph Parker, born in 1992, won the WBO heavyweight championship title, beating Andy Ruiz in 2016. He lost the title to Briton Anthony Joshua in March 2018.

Equine

New Zealand's climate has played a major part in the development of thoroughbred and standardbred horse breeding with many champions produced since missionary Samuel Marsden brought the animals to the country in 1814.

Among the most famous of New Zealand's equine champions were Phar Lap, a crowd favourite during the Great Depression of the 1930s, and Cardigan Bay, a New Zealand harness racer that became the first standardbred to win more than US$1 million, winning races in New Zealand, Australia and North America.

Chapter Ten

NOTABLE FIRSTS

Circa 1300
The first Polynesians settled in New Zealand, ancestors of the Maori people.

1642
Dutch explorer Abel Tasman sighted New Zealand for the first time but didn't land.

1769
British explorer James Cook visited New Zealand for the first time.

1806
The first women arrived from Europe.

1815
The first pakeha child, Thomas Holloway King, was born in New Zealand.

1837
The first possum arrived in New Zealand from Australia.

1840
Russell, in the Bay of Islands, became New Zealand's first capital.

Taxation was introduced, initially for some imported products, and for legal documents such as mortgages.

1842

Maketu Wharetotara was the first person executed by hanging in New Zealand, for the murder of two adults and five children.

1854

Parliament met for the first time, in Auckland.

1859

New Zealand's first lighthouse, at Wellington's Pencarrow Head, lit up for the first time.

1862

Dunedin was the first city to get reticulated water.

1862

The country's first telegraph line operated between Christchurch and Lyttleton.

Professional opera made its debut with a performance by a visiting troupe from England in Dunedin.

1863

The first steam railway began operating.

1864

Elizabeth Yates was elected Mayor of Onehunga, becoming the first woman mayor in the British Empire.

1865

Auckland streets were lit by gas for the first time.

The first session of Parliament was held in Wellington, the new country's new capital, after re-location from Auckland.

Stamp and death duties were passed into law.

1869

New Zealand's first university, the University of Otago, took its first students.

Hamiora Pere became the first (and last) New Zealander to be hanged for treason.

1870

The first game of rugby was played in New Zealand.

The first meat exported to Britain was packed in 842 cases of cans.

1876

The national anthem, *God Defend New Zealand*, was performed in public for the first time on Christmas Day in Dunedin.

1877

The first New Zealand telephone call was made between telegraph offices in Dunedin and Milton.

The passing of the Education Act established the country's first compulsory and free system of primary education.

1882

Christchurch was the first city with a sewerage system, built to defeat typhoid.

The first tourist guidebook to New Zealand was published.

Frozen sheep carcasses were exported by ship to Britain for the first time.

1886

Oil was first discovered in Taranaki.

1887

The first inland parcel was delivered by the postal services.

1888

The coal-mining town of Reefton on the West Coast of the South Island was the first to get reticulated electricity.

1889

New Zealand's first sci-fi novel was published - *Anno Domini 2000; or a Woman's Destiny*, written by former Premier Sir Julius Vogel.

1893

New Zealand women became the first in the world to be given the right to vote.

1894

The government bailed out the Bank of New Zealand for the first time, preventing it from going broke.

Julius Vogel. Photo: Archives New Zealand (Creative Commons licence).

Climbers reached the summit of Aoraki/Mt Cook, New Zealand's highest peak, for the first time.

1895

Minnie Dean became the first (and only) woman hanged in New Zealand for murder.

1896

Moving pictures were screened for the first time, during a night of vaudeville at the Opera House, Auckland.

1898

The first imported cars, two vehicles made by Benz, appeared on New Zealand streets.

Photographer W.H.Bartlett shot the first motion picture in New Zealand.

1901

The population of the North Island exceeded that of the South Island for the first time.

1903

On March 31, Richard Pearse flew his home-made aircraft 150 metres, arguably becoming the world's first aviator.

1908

New Zealand's population reached one million.

The first train travelled the length of the North Island when 680km of main trunk line was opened.

1909

The world's first stamp-vending machine was invented and made in New Zealand.

1910

The first coin-operated telephones were installed.

1912

Swimmer Malcolm Champion became the first New Zealander to win an Olympic gold medal.

1914

The country's first feature film was made, telling the legend of Hinemoa.

Auckland finally got its first water reticulation and sewerage systems, the last of the main centres to get them.

1916

Vivian Walsh became the first New Zealand pilot licensed to fly.

1917

The first time that licensed premises were required to close by 6pm — the start of what became known as 'the six o'clock swill' as workers crammed into bars after work.

1920

The first flight across Cook Strait delivered the first air mail between the two islands.

Fingerprint evidence helped convict a murderer in Auckland, claimed to be a world first.

1925

The introduction of car registrations saw the first steel number plates.

1926 The Radio Broadcasting Company began regular public broadcasts.

Clocks were changed to New Zealand Summer Time for the first time.

1928

Aviator Charles Kingsford Smith completed the first flight across the Tasman Sea.

1932

The first coins with distinctly New Zealand markings went into circulation.

1933

Elizabeth McCombs was elected the country's first woman MP.

E.F ('Teddy') Harvie became the first pilot to fly the 1880km journey from North Cape to Bluff in a single day.

1937

The government introduced free milk into schools (a scheme that ended in 1967).

New Zealand's first State house was opened in Miramar, Wellington. Photo: Archives New Zealand (Creative Commons licence).

The first State house was opened as part of a scheme to provide affordable housing for New Zealanders.

1938

The first official New Zealand airmail was delivered to the United States.

1944

Coca-Cola began local manufacture in New Zealand.

1947

Mabel Howard became New Zealand's first woman cabinet minister.

The NZ Symphony Orchestra made its debut performance.

1949

New Zealand's navy got its first four frigates.

1951

Government regulations allowed the first local manufacture of yogurt.

1952

New Zealand's population reached two million.

1953

On May 29, New Zealand mountaineer Edmund Hillary with Sherpa Tenzing Norga became the first men to conquer the summit of Mt Everest, the world's highest mountain.

The newly-crowned Queen Elizabeth visited New Zealand with Prince Philip, the first time a reigning monarch had visited.

1958

The government introduced PAYE income tax.

The first heart-lung machine was used at Green Lane Hospital, Auckland.

Pepsi-Cola was available for the first time in New Zealand.

1959

The first vehicles crossed the Auckland Harbour Bridge.

1960

The first television programme was broadcast.

The Treasury leased an IBM Mainframe computer, the first computer to be used in the country.

Changes to the Licensing Act allowed the first licensed restaurants.

1961

The Griffins biscuit factory became the first commercial user of a computer.

1962

New Zealand signed its first trade pact with Japan.

Barrie Devenport became the first person to swim Cook Strait.

1965

New Zealand took its first steps to free trade with Australia by signing the NZ–Australia Free Trade Agreement (NAFTA).

1966

The National Library opened.

1967

The country used decimal currency for the first time, replacing pounds, shillings and pence with dollars and cents.

Traffic authorities began using breath and blood tests to combat drunk drivers.

New Zealanders could legally drink on licensed premises till 10pm for the first time as a referendum brought an end to six o'clock closing.

1972

The first container shipping service began between New Zealand and the United Kingdom.

Table margarine became available for sale.

1973

The Great Ngaruawahia Music Festival became the country's first significant outdoor music event, attracting 18,000.

New Zealand's population reached three million.

Angela D'Audney became the first woman to read the news on national television.

New Zealand joined the Organisation for Economic Co-operation and Development (OECD).

The first television programmes were transmitted in colour.

1974

New Zealand introduced its accident compensation scheme to provide no-fault personal accident insurance cover for its citizens.

Retired public servant Dr William B. Sutch was the first New Zealander prosecuted under the 1951 Official Secrets Act. He was eventually acquitted.

1975

The country's second television channel began transmission.

The Cook Strait was conquered for the first time by a woman swimmer, American Lynne Cox.

1976

The first McDonald's fast food store opened in Porirua, Wellington.

1977

The National Superannuation scheme started.

The 200 nautical mile exclusive economic zone (EEZ) was established, preventing foreign fishing boats from legally taking fish from New Zealand waters.

The Queen approved *God Defend New Zealand*, giving it equal status for the first time (with *God Save The Queen*) as the national anthem.

1979

The first Automatic Teller Machine (ATM) was installed at a bank.

1980

Shops opened for legal trading on Saturday for the first time after decades of operating solely Monday to Friday (with some late night shopping).

1983

Australia and New Zealand agreed to free trade between their countries through the Closer Economic Relations (CER) Agreement.

1984
The first EFTPOS machine was used in a retail store.
1985
The first case of locally-contracted AIDS was reported.

The New Zealand dollar's value was set by international markets for the first time when it was floated, becoming known as the Kiwi.

The number of annual tourists exceeded half a million.
1986
Shoppers paid Goods and Services Tax (GST) for the first time.

The Pope made the first papal visit to New Zealand.
1987
The first draw was held for Lotto, the country's national lottery.

The country's first heart transplant operation was performed in Auckland.
1988
The world's first commercial bungy jump operation opened at Kawarau Bridge in the South Island.
1989
After years of restricting opening hours to six days a week, retailers accepted Sunday trading and introduced seven-day shopping.
1990
Sky TV launched its pay-TV channels offering movies, sport and news on UHF.

Dr Penny Jamieson became the first female Anglican bishop in New Zealand, and the world.
1994
The country's first licensed casino opened in Christchurch.

Actress Anna Paquin was the first New Zealander to win an Oscar for acting.

1998
Sky TV launched the first digital satellite television service.

1999
Georgina Beyer became New Zealand's first transgender MP.

2003
New Zealand's population reached four million.

2004
The first same-sex marriages became recognised in law with the passing of the Civil Union Act.

2007
The KiwiSaver retirement scheme was introduced.

Corporal Willie Apiata became the first recipient of the New Zealand Victoria Cross.

2015
Golfer Lydia Ko became the first New Zealander to be ranked No. 1 in the world, aged 17.

2018
Prime Minister Jacinda Ardern became the first elected head of a New Zealand government to give birth while in office.

2021
New Zealand's population reached 5 million.

ABOUT THE AUTHOR

Peter Jessup

THE AUTHOR is a veteran New Zealand journalist whose work has appeared in major newspapers such as the *New Zealand Herald* and *Auckland Star*, as well as leading magazines. Passionate about New Zealand's history, Jessup delighted in enlightening others about the ways of his country until his death in late 2018.

Jessup's other books include *Fishermen's Tales* and *Boaties' Tales*, both published by Hurricane Press.

Publisher's note: This edition has been updated by our editors since Peter Jessup's death.

MORE NEW ZEALAND BOOKS

Other Hurricane Press titles include:

INSTANT! MAORI, by Nick Theobald and Paul (Paaora) Walker

The fun, street-wise Maori-English phrase book that enables you to start speaking Maori in seconds! This ebook helps you with etiquette on the marae (Maori meeting house), making introductions and using many everyday words and phrases. The authors' sense of humour ensures this book will put a smile on your face as you learn.

MYTH NEW ZEALAND: All the stories from Series One, by Justin Brown

Justin Brown sets out to discover whether modern New Zealand is the same place he was promised when growing up in the 1970s - the land of rugby, racing and beer, 80 million sheet and number 8 fencing wire. Brown performs a 21st century reality check, seeking to learn whether the land of his birth is still the best place to bring up kids and what the future might hold for its citizens.

STRANGER THAN FICTION: The Life and Times of Split Enz, by Mike Chunn

One of the founders of New Zealand's most successful rock band, Splitz Enz, reveals the inside story behind their often-chaotic assault on the music world.

FISHERMEN'S TALES, by Peter Jessup

Everyone likes a fishy story and veteran fishing writer Jessup has been collecting them for more than 30 years. *Fishermen's Tales* is a collection of his favourite stories from the streams and coastlines of New Zealand, to the rivers, lakes and seas around the world. As incredible as these stories seem, all of them are true. Honest.

BOATIES' TALES, by Peter Jessup

Amazing stories from the world of boating - about yachts, tankers, fishing trawlers or the humble dinghy - as Jessup sets out to prove the happiest two days in a boat-owner's life are the day he buys the boat and the day he sells it.

HOOK: One man's search for the perfect day's fishing, by Anthony Swainson

The first in a trilogy of fishing story collections in which the author travels the world in search of the perfect day's fishing.

LINE: One man's search for the perfect day's fishing, by Anthony Swainson

Second book in the trilogy.

SINKER: One man's search for the perfect day's fishing, by Anthony Swainson

Third book in the trilogy.

HOOK, LINE & SINKER: One man's search for the perfect day's fishing, by Anthony Swainson

This is a compilation of all the stories in Anthony Swainson's trilogy, and includes an extra chapter in which he describes his final day's fishing after sixty years of landing fish.

LANDED: One man's search for the perfect day's fishing, by Anthony Swainson

Not content with his trilogy, Anthony Swainson finds more stories from his fishing locker to delight his fans.

<u>Hurricane Press</u>
Cambridge
New Zealand

Printed in Great Britain
by Amazon